From One Man's Dream

by Judith Irving • illustrated by Den Schofield

Harcourt

Orlando Boston Dallas Chicago San Diego

Visit *The Learning Site!*

www.harcourtschool.com

Learning is something that can happen anywhere and at any time of life. Sometimes it is life itself that does the teaching, though it takes a wise person to decipher the lesson. That is what happened to Franklin Delano Roosevelt when he was already 39 years old, a man with a career and a family. It was a lesson that began on an August day in 1921.

Illness Strikes

FDR, as he was known, was a very determined man who hated to give in to any kind of weakness. On that summer day, FDR was doing two important things. One was playing with and entertaining his children, and the other was trying to recover from three years of hard work without a real rest.

The family's beautiful vacation home was set in a place that was perfect for both purposes. Campobello is on the eastern shore of Canada near Maine. On August 10, FDR had already helped put out a forest fire he and the children had spotted while sailing. Then everyone had gone for a swim. However, FDR was still feeling tired. He decided that what he needed to overcome that tired feeling was even more exercise, so he and the children jogged a couple of miles, then cooled off with yet another swim in icy waters.

When he got back to the house, FDR did not change out of his bathing suit right away. Instead, he sat reading the mail that had been delivered while he was out. When he finally went upstairs, he was still feeling sick, so he climbed into bed, hoping to avoid the cold he thought he was getting.

The next morning, FDR had a fever. After a couple of days, he was even worse. At first he had pain in his back and legs, but before long he could not walk or even move his legs. For a while, even his hands and arms were paralyzed; he could not move them. FDR's wife, Eleanor, stayed close by his side, helping him in every way she could.

At first, nobody knew for sure what was wrong with FDR. It was not until August 25 that the family learned that he had polio, and there was no real cure. The only thing that might help, said the doctor, was hot baths.

FDR enjoyed being in public service, and many people thought he would go far in politics. He had already served in the government as Assistant Secretary of the Navy. He had also run for Vice President of the United States. Though his party lost that election, many people felt that FDR would have other chances. After all, his distant cousin, Theodore Roosevelt, had been the twenty-sixth President, and FDR was married to Theodore's niece. Politics definitely ran in the family.

FDR also loved boats and ships, and he loved the water, which was one reason he had enjoyed being Assistant Secretary of the Navy. Yet here he was, unable to move his legs. How would he be able to continue in the kind of life he had planned?

FDR's early life had been the type only children of wealthy families could enjoy. He never went to public school, but was taught by either a governess or a tutor until he was fourteen. After that he went to classes in a private school. By then he was already able to speak French and German.

After graduation, he went on to Harvard University, where he rowed, played football, and was an editor of the *Harvard Crimson*, the school newspaper. Still, though he had grown up with everything that money could buy, he also remembered his father's lessons. James Roosevelt always taught his son that being wealthy came with a responsibility—to help others who were not as lucky. It was a lesson that would, in the months that followed, be reinforced by FDR's illness.

Some things soon became clear about the way FDR would behave with regard to his disease. First, he was determined to recover full use of his legs. Second, he did not want to be treated any differently by others, even though he had to depend on help from many people. Third, also with the help of others, he would keep the seriousness of his disability secret from the public.

Returning to Politics

Eleanor Roosevelt understood that it was important to keep up her husband's spirits. She felt that he needed to be interested and active in public life. That was the only way he would recover or at least overcome his limits. So she encouraged FDR's interest in politics.

Sara Roosevelt, FDR's mother, had other ideas. She wanted her son to retire from public life as an invalid and not be active at all. She did not understand that FDR would not be able to stand the immobility.

In the end, Eleanor won out. FDR's political career did not end. He kept in touch with his friends and supporters in public life and continued to fight his disease. After a time, he recovered the use of his hands. Though he still could not move his legs and feet, he exercised every day to develop strength in his arms and shoulders. He even learned to walk again, but he could do so only with the help of heavy metal braces on his legs.

Swimming was especially good for FDR, and he did it as often as he could. He would say, "The water put me where I am, and the water has to bring me back." He was referring, of course, to that last swim he had before becoming paralyzed.

Finally, FDR decided to return to politics. The public had been informed that he'd had a mild case of polio, from which he was recovering. FDR made up his mind that he would always try to appear in public standing on his own two feet. He would depend on crutches and the braces to keep him upright. Though he used a wheelchair in private, he wanted that part of his life to be kept out of the public eye.

In 1924, he was asked to go to the Democratic convention to nominate Al Smith for President. FDR worked very hard to be able to walk out on the platform with the help of his son Jimmy. As people were applauding his speech, he shouted to a friend, "I made it! I made it!"

Warm Springs

It was about this time that FDR heard about a man with polio who had recovered the use of his legs by swimming in the naturally hot pools of Warm Springs, Georgia. The temperature of the water that flowed out of the ground was 88 degrees. FDR decided to try it.

Right from the start, FDR found that the water at the resort relaxed him. The best part was that he could actually stand on his own in the pool. Then one day there was a real change. For the first time since he had been sick, FDR could feel life in his toes. Now he was sure that he would recover the use of his legs.

Even with this improvement, though, FDR saw that, to his dismay, his recovery would take much longer than he had hoped. This would have been hard for FDR to accept even if he had not been the kind of man he was. Yet his illness had begun to change him. He was learning how important time and patience were to his recovery.

His wife Eleanor saw an even greater change in her husband's personality. She said of him that his struggle with polio turned out to be "a blessing in disguise," for he had found in himself a new strength and courage. Also, he was now a more caring man, with more sympathy for others' problems.

That change was clear in what he decided to do about Warm Springs. FDR was a public figure, and newspapers spread the word that he was doing well there. Already one leg was improving, and he could walk a few hundred feet by using crutches and wearing a brace only on his left leg. Now others wanted to come to the resort at Warm Springs as well. FDR used his own money to build a second pool for other polio victims.

However, the resort where he was staying was not doing well financially. FDR decided that there was only one thing to do: buy the place himself. Against his mother's advice, he spent two-thirds of his own money to buy the resort. Then he set up the Georgia Warm Springs Foundation. The goal of the foundation was to treat polio victims and help them recover, just as FDR felt he was recovering.

Mr. President

In 1928, Al Smith, the governor of New York, was running again for the presidency, which he had failed to win four years earlier. He wanted FDR to run for governor of New York in his place. At first FDR turned Smith down. He wanted to spend more time on improving his health. He also wanted to make sure that the Warm Springs project would succeed. After all, it had cost a great deal of his fortune. Finally, though, FDR agreed to run.

He knew that some people despised him and his ideas. Those people were spreading the rumor that because of polio, he would not be able to travel during the political campaign. To prove them wrong, FDR traveled all over the state. He managed, with the help of others, to hide from the public how severely polio had affected him. News photographers, for example, did not take pictures of him except when he was seated or managing to move on his own.

FDR was elected easily. Then, after four years as governor, he ran for President. The country was in a deep depression, with millions of people out of work. FDR was elected the thirty-second President of the United States on the promise that he would improve things for all Americans.

FDR went on to be elected four times in all, more than any other President. During that time, the United States fought a world war on two fronts, in Europe and in Asia. The length of his political career probably astonished the people who once thought that a weakened FDR would not be able to continue in politics.

Finding a Cure

Even with all the campaigning and presidential duties, FDR continued to swim and exercise. As President he would start each day with a swim in the White House pool. He returned to Warm Springs as often as he could. It had become like a second home to him. In fact, his summer home there was known as the Little White House.

FDR went to Warm Springs for more than the healing waters. He also enjoyed its peaceful atmosphere and the community of people who gathered there. He could get away, if only for a little while, from politics and from the war. He liked to tell people about the legend of Warm Springs. It was said that years ago wounded fighters from different Native American nations used to come to the springs to heal themselves. Even though they were enemies, in that one place at least, there was peace and healing.

Nor did he ever forget the other polio patients there and elsewhere in the world. Every year on January 30, his birthday, FDR held a Presidential Ball in Washington, D.C. The money raised was donated to a national foundation to aid new polio victims and help researchers find a cure for the disease. It also helped continue the rehabilitation work done at Warm Springs.

Fundraising for the polio foundation went on all over the country. It was still the Depression, though, and many people could give only small coins. Eddie Cantor, a well-known performer, came up with a name for the foundation: the March of Dimes. The name stuck.

FDR, worn out from illness and the war, died in office in 1945, but the effort to cure polio went on and finally succeeded. In the 1950s, American researchers developed two different polio vaccines. That great achievement reduced the number of new cases so much that a special place for polio victims was no longer needed. Instead of closing, though, the Warm Springs Foundation expanded its work to help people with all kinds of disabilities.

Over time, the state of Georgia became more and more involved in the medical program at Warm Springs. By 1980 it had taken it over. The Roosevelt Warm Springs Institute for Rehabilitation, as it is now known, serves more than 5,000 people a year. Its goal is to bring everyone, no matter what his or her disability, into the mainstream of life. The Institute includes such services as a Center for Therapeutic Recreation. The center has a basketball court, pool, and bowling alley. Then there is Camp Dream, which serves young campers, with a lake for fishing and swimming.

It is, all in all, Franklin Delano Roosevelt's dream come true.